The Optimist's Truth

Ed Lee

BookLeaf Publishing

India | USA | UK

Presentation by *BookLeaf Publishing*

Web: www.bookleafpub.com

E-mail: info@bookleafpub.com

ISBN: 9789358313482

First edition 2023

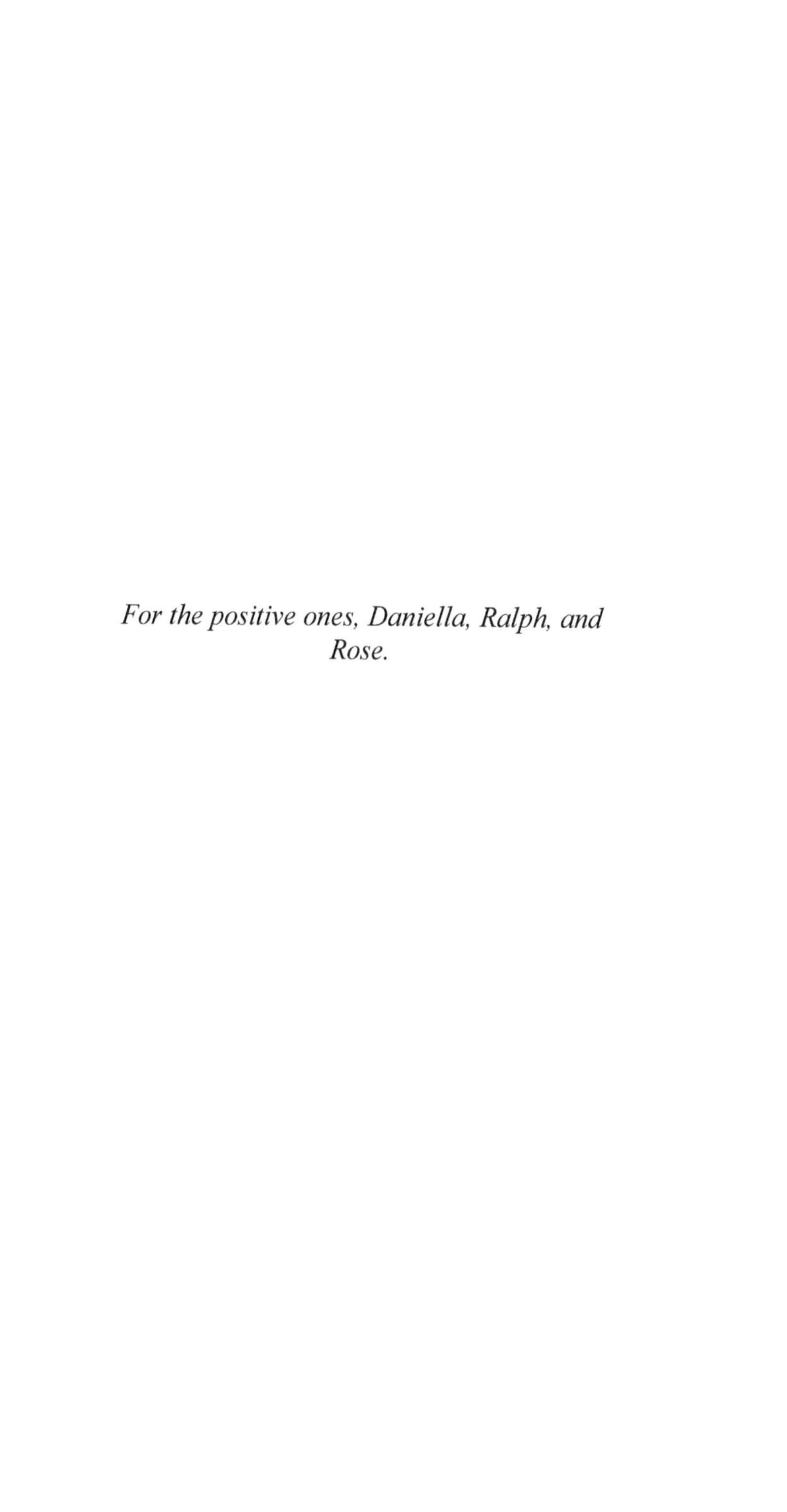

For the positive ones, Daniella, Ralph, and Rose.

ACKNOWLEDGEMENT

Thank you to TJ for being my biggest supporter, my proof-reader, and for always pushing me to write more.

Oh, Sobriety

Oh, sobriety, how I loathe thee,
The audacity of responsibility;
Financial stability, housework, maturity.
The cruel monotony of reliability;
Alarms, speed limits and fuel economy.
Repeat, repeat, repeat.
The daily grind wearing our fingers to the bone.
Slowly.
Continuously.
Terminally.

Sombre moods, fuelled by targets and service,
broken by achievements and the reward of
ownership. One goal, to get out of here alive,
destined to fail from the start.

Escape to a hazy world, a dreamland filled with
laughter and friendship, where conversations
twist and turn like a river, everlasting, free
flowing.
A return to self.

Golden sunlight beams down, warming the
bodies and souls.

Endless evenings; adventures, stories shared
with strangers.
Enveloped by a warm embrace, a renewed sense
of being. More than pure existence.
We are alive.
Time spent now is valuable, not expensive.
Bonds are formed, stronger than any weld.
Friends in the present, family in the future.
No escape, no need to escape. Happiness as far
as the mind's eye can see.
Unbreakable.
For now, forever.

Alarm, work, hangover.

Oh, sobriety, how I loathe thee.

All of This

On these country lanes we're free to be whatever
we will choose
To hide beneath the darkness of an ever waning
moon
The tarmac rivers lead us from humanity behind
But we'll try our very best to be forgotten over
time.

There's nothing left for us in the time that we
have had
It's just countless different endings to be drawn
out of a hat
Take my joy, my hope, my empathy, and lash it
to the fence
So some lost soul, who's cast away, can try and
find some sense

In all of this.
There's something we can learn
In all of this.
Before our futures burn
In all of this.
Before our faith expires
We can't resist.

Just one more chance to show the world how we
almost won

So grab a pen and draw a thousand words on
paper hats
We'll wear them when we celebrate just how
much time has passed
We'll frame your pictures, keep your memories
stored inside a box
Safely locked away so you'll forget that we are
lost

Between the Stars

5

I tried to open up a hole between the stars for
you
Where we could sit and watch the universe
expand before our eyes

You took the stars and made them brighter than
they'd ever been
You rearranged the galaxies to show me all that
you had seen

The space between the cells divides us from the
things we've felt
I ache to see inside your head and open thoughts
that I misread

Beneath the surface lies a truth that only you
will know
You'll mask the fear behind a gaze, and smile
through the hardest days

I will always be me
And you have always been truth

Smile

I never had the strength to say
How much you really mean to me
I've always been a coward in that respect

I know that I can never make
Amends for my mistakes, but I
Intend to show you I can be a better man

I never really thought that I
Would find someone who makes me smile
Half as much as I find that you do

A thousand words cannot explain
The guilt I feel, for all the pain
That I've caused you and I cannot repair

So let me take you by the hand
And lead you through the labyrinth of my mind
I'll guide you through the bolted doors
And shelter you from all the storms
Eating away slowly at my soul

If I get lost along the way
I hope I never hear you say
That it's because I just do not care

I have my faults I can't deny
And though it's me who's made you cry
I promise I'll do my best to make you smile

No Direction

It's been less than what I hoped for
Here I am, feeling so unsure
I can't help but get the feeling
That someone has set me up
I am lost with no direction
I'm not losing my momentum
I don't know what I'm supposed to do
I guess I never thought this through

Bruises

The faded bruises on your arms draw me in
Each one tells a story, tainting your pale skin
Hiding a truth you won't share

There's so much more to you than the surface
will surrender
Your past runs deep and ragged, and hides the
beauty of your mind

Such mystery surrounds you
My desire to know more leads me into fantasy
You're an arm's length away, and I can't get
closer

Let me find out more
Confess your fears, dictate your dreams
Watch your life play out before my eyes
I see the breath rise in your chest
Then fall away in silent theft
It's my imagination, nothing more
An empty room
A sealed door
I can see the light inside

I trace the lines across your face

You're nowhere to be seen
But you are here with me

A fading vision of another life
The heat from your hands
Burning through my clothes

The hairs stand upright, my neck constricting
I see your name
On all the walls in all the rooms
You never give me peace
I try to get away, but I just can't turn down your
noise
The bruises will never truly fade

The Optimist's Truth

You can give it all away
Or you can keep it close to your chest
The thoughts that seem simple
Are only simple until they're expressed

Try as you might to adjust
You'll never be quite good enough
Give it up and move along
Just try and find something new

The optimist will spend his life drowning
In a pool of his own naivety
Lost without the courage to admit
That it's time to accept his defeat

Rather than living a lie
Stop pretending that everything's fine
As your life crumbles away
Just admit it to yourself

Slip Away

The times when I'm left thinking
Of the days we spent conspiring
Are the days I find I'm wishing that
All of this will never change

I'm foolish and a dreamer
And I know it might not seem it
But I'm longing for a comfort
From something I've never seen

You're hurting on the inside
And can't hide as well as you'd like
But your heavy arms are aching
And your head's hung in despair

This isn't it
We can be so much more
Our hands are raw and aching
From holding on too tightly
To what we can't afford to lose
Don't let it slip
Don't let it slip away

Low

Watching faces as they pass
The distant loneliness
The rain runs down the glass
As the present turns to past
The moments that should last
Lost forever in a flash
But the memories live on
The memories live on

The weakness in the morning
And the pain throughout the day
Is a simple harsh reminder
That will never go away
The sticks and stones that others throw
Are a blessing in disguise
They cover tracks and help distract
From what burns deep inside

And if I had a penny
For every time that I felt low
I would have been a millionaire
So many years ago
But the things I would have missed
And the folks I'd never met
Would have made for an existence
That's so easy to forget

Telling Tales

In a life where every second counts
You chose an early exit
To you the world was a lonely place
Where no-one knew your face
You sat alone in darkened rooms
Trying to make sense
Of all the things that have passed before
And lead you to this point

Perhaps things could have been different
If only for one small detail
A misplaced word
A misread smile
Could change the path of life
Or maybe it goes deeper
And would be harder to correct
Are the paths we take set in our blood
From the moment we are born?

You often wondered why
People seem so cold
There's despair in your eyes and on your face
But nobody seems to recognise
Speaking out is hard to do
To make the first move and ask for help

If only someone would step up
And offer you their hand

Things could have been so different
It didn't have to end this way
You never wanted it to
But now we'll never know

Age of Denial

Why don't we pretend
That we haven't spent
The last 10 years
Growing older on the outside

Maybe if we close our eyes
Then we can go back
To a better time
And we'll never age another day again

I want to be the one
Who can change the way you feel
Who can stop you in your tracks
And make your dreams seem real
It's like we've never met
But I know just who you are
There's nothing I can say
That will let you down
Or make you think
That this has gone too far

Will you sing songs to me
About the heart
That you feel breaking
And the lies you always told

It doesn't have to end
We'll just take
The mature approach
And deny this ever happened to us

Not Your Fight

So cast your critic's eye
Over all that you despise
You don't have the strength inside you
Just to let it lie

You refuse to see the damage
You caused aiming your gun
Directly at the heart
Of the man that you once loved

Take away your sharpened daggers
And cloak of twisted faith
The place for you has fallen
And your loyalties replaced
With poisoned tongues
And bitter hands
That tell of secrets never read
Fuelled by rejection
From someone you've never met

The mask you wear
Will give you strength
And help you justify defence
As you wage war on common sense

The deeper you appear to sink
The darker thoughts you start to think
Until you find yourself confused
And you turn into the accused

Stay out of this
It's not your fight
You don't need to be heard
Just because you think you're right
It's not your fight

Forgotten Friends

Do you ever stop to think
How many people come and go
Disappear into the past
Lost in the ebb and flow

Each one a character
In the chapter of the present
The pages turning faster
An uncontrollable descent

The lights behind the eyes
Slowly flicker and fade to black
An empty shell left standing
Without ever looking back

A scar in time for each
And every one another line
The images so vivid
Become forgotten over time

But sparks remain to re-ignite
The way we used to feel
The promise of new hope
We once believed was real

The Painful Act of Growing Up

Everyone's so desperate
For us to grow up
But what really happens
When we grow up?

We fall into our routines
We lose the love for what matters
The weight of expectations
Dragging us down, towards the grave

Youth isn't wasted on the young
Regret's a curse that's learnt with age

It's hard not to put your faith in
All that has gone before
When the future seems destined to be destroyed

It's so easy to look back and wish

It never seemed so easy then
But looking back
To start over again

We wouldn't waste a day

Or let it slip past again
We'd make the most of it
The second time around

It's easy to fall into the grooves
That the others carve for us
Out of the wood
That we spend our lives
Polishing every single mark out of
Hoping it's up to scratch

Suddenly you notice
Without a flinch
How many years have passed
Since you let yourself dream

Soaking through your skin
Like the blood through your torn jeans
You see the shame that you feel
From letting your life pass you by

Sometimes

Sometimes
It's not that I don't like you
But tonight I want to fight you
To see you standing by the door
Not knowing whether to stay

Sometimes
It's not that I'm unhappy
I just feel far from happy
When I think about the ways in which
You make me want to stay

Sometimes
It isn't just the bad times
That can bring on all of the sad times
I just find that everything can be
Somewhat overwhelming

Sometimes
I just don't want to see you
But I do still need to feel you
To know that you'll be there
When the worst of times have passed

Every Moment

Every moment hurts
As you lose everything
Someone, somewhere
Is gaining everything
It's easy to forget
In times of happiness
What every moment
Might mean to someone else
Yet we live our lives
In a state of ignorance
The only thing we all share
And we cannot change
Is that at some point
This will come to an end
And there is nothing
Nothing to soften the blow

The Fear

It's consequence that frightens us the most
Don't you know
In restraints with nowhere to run
Can't you see
You're alone, left to freeze
You feel lost
Close your eyes, scared to breathe

Take a leap and jump straight in
The fear of never knowing
Will forever haunt your sleep
Don't be left behind in a life that never stops
It's time to be a hero
Step up and save yourself

Can't deny what you feel inside
In a trap
Weighed down, holding on
All you've got
Fight off, cut the ties
Find the light
Start to run and don't look back

So you're standing alone on the bridge
Contemplating gravity

You let your mind wander
But don't let it stray too far
There's a chance it may never come back

Pieces of You

I found you in your living room
As far from living as could ever be
You had a life before this
But I find it so hard to believe

A life stacked neatly into piles
In a room encased in death
Passed between the present and the past
I cannot bear to see the rest

The emptiness that I have felt
Will never match that which you are in
I search for you in the dark
And know I will never see the truth

There's something in the order of decay
That brings a sense of meaning to the day
That I got to know you in this way
And questioned all that I had ever seen

The pieces of you that we have left
Do nothing to justify the loss
Of everything that you have left behind
As the world shifts to fill the void

Thoughts Sublime

We don't talk the way we used to
Anymore
We're both lost in our own worlds
So unsure

There's nothing left to fill the space
So vast and cold

It hasn't been the same for years
Both so alone
Only share the air we breathe
So monochrome

There's nothing left to fill the space
So vast and cold
You face away to hide regrets
You never told

We once believed it
Could never see it
So rose tinted
But never meant it

Why did we let it come to this
So far apart

Used to share our thoughts sublime
Back at the start

Say I'm Right

You look to me when I say that I am right
I will always say I'm right
It's up to you who you choose to believe
No one's forcing your hand

I heard you lost everything that you loved
And now you search for it all
Along the streets paved with glitter and blood
You're just retracing your steps

Into the night you will walk in your shoes
They've walked a thousand miles before
They'll tear your feet to shreds and bring you to
tears
But you just keep pressing on

I hope that you can find what you're searching
for
Make yourself complete again
I'll bring the torch that I've been burning for
years
And I will help to guide you home

Was it Better?

I'm mourning the death of the life that we had
Before everything changed for the better
When time was our own and was all we had
known
And it's hard to say that wasn't better

Not nearly enough to call it regret
But enough to write an epitaph
For the people we were and the things that we
felt
Now it's time to leave them behind

I squint through the fog of eternal exhaustion,
That has settled over my eyes
From lack of sleep and from lack of peace
And from lack of self too clear to hide

I'll still love you until I die
The joy that I see in your eye
Makes everything else feel fine
As I softly decay inside

I'm mourning the death of the life that we had
Before everything changed for the better

To see that we've grown, from what we had
known
I'll say things were different, not better